POWER POINTS FOR TODAY'S BUSY BELIEVER

A 30-DAY DEVOTIONAL THAT MEETS YOU AT YOUR SCHEDULE

By James D. Holiday Sr.

Copyright © 2018 by JDH Ministries

Power Points For Today's Busy Believer

by James D. Holiday, Sr.

ISBN-13: 978-1726397520 1st print edition

All rights reserved. No part of this book may be reproduced, stored in a retrieval system, or transmitted in any form or by any means electronic, mechanical, photocopy, recording, or any other—except for brief quotations in printed reviews, without the prior written consent of the publisher. If you purchase this book without a cover you should be aware that this book may have been stolen property and reported as "unsold and destroyed" to the Publisher. In such case neither the author nor the publisher has received any payment for this "stripped book."Scripture quotations marked (KJV) are taken from the Holy Bible, Copyright © 1973, 1978, 1984 by Biblica, Inc. ™ Used by permission of Zondervan. All rights reserved worldwide.

Table of Contents

The Official Reset!..DAY 1

Guard Your Heart! ....DAY 2

Discipline Yourself!...DAY 3

No Worries..DAY 4

Activate Your Faith Today! ....DAY 5

Supernatural Supply Is Your Portion!..................................DAY 6

You Will Finish Strong!...DAY 7

Integrity Has To Be Priority! ....DAY 8

You're Loaded! ....DAY 9

Adopt A Breakthrough Mindset!..DAY 10

Contentment Is The Key! ....DAY 11

A Time Of Completion! ....DAY 12

Submit To What He's Doing!..DAY 13

Set Your Mind On Right Things! ....DAY 14

Do The Right Thing! ....DAY 15

What's Your "WHY"? ....DAY 16

Have You Responded To That Word Yet?........................DAY 17

Embrace Correction And Make The Adjustment! ....DAY 18

Keep It Real With Yourself!..DAY 19

It's Ok To Tweak Some Things! ....DAY 20

There's Always Room For Better!.....................................DAY 21

Time To Live A Limitless Life!..DAY 22

Embrace The Potter's Wheel!...DAY 23

The Potential Of Prayer! ....DAY 24

Spirit Of Fear: Declaration & Confession! ....DAY 25

Prayer and Decree Against Depression & Suicide! ....DAY 26

Scriptures and Decrees For FOCUS! ....DAY 27

Authority! ....DAY 28

Prayer Is Your Foundation! ....DAY 29

Birth Your Own! ....DAY 30

DAY 1
The Official RESET!

1. PRIORITIES

Matthew 6:33 But seek ye first the kingdom of God, and his righteousness; and all these things shall be added unto you.

(The Father must be highest priority in every aspect of your life; starting now!)

2. PERSUIT

Psalm 119:10 **With my whole heart have I sought thee: O let me not wander from thy commandments.**

3. PERSISTANCE

Galatians 6:9 **And let us not be weary in well doing: for in due season we shall reap, if we faint not.**

(Often times doing the will of God will invite opposition; you must position yourself to maintain)

Make it your business to align your days with the plans of God. Let today be the day you begin to occupy your God ordained position!

DAY 2
Guard Your Heart!

Refuse to be a slave to other people's dysfunction. Control and manipulation can come in through feelings that are not policed properly. GAURD YOUR HEART!!

Proverbs 4:23 **Keep thy heart with all diligence; for out of it are the issues of life.**

You have a responsibility to govern your Peace, Place & Purpose. Sometimes people, even those you love, need help honoring and respecting your space and boundaries.

DAY 3
Discipline Yourself!

Develop a daily system and make yourself accountable to it.

- ❖ New disciplines- Commit to doing & not doing certain things!
- ❖ New standards- Safe guard your integrity. What will you accept?
- ❖ New levels of self-control- Govern your appetites & impulses.

Proverbs 25:28 **He that hath no rule over his own spirit is like a city that is broken down, and without walls.**

DAY 4
No Worries!

Don't worry about anything! Pray about everything! Bring yourself to a place of assurance today knowing that what you see may not be what is.

Philippians 4:6-7

⁶Be careful for nothing; but in everything by prayer and supplication with thanksgiving let your requests be made known unto God.

⁷And the peace of God, which passeth all understanding, shall keep your hearts and minds through Christ Jesus.

Worrying impregnates your mind with doubt and accelerates procrastination. Everything that opens you up for that spirit must be dealt with swiftly and aggressively.

DAY 5
Activate Your Faith Today!

How can you successfully make the biggest move you've ever made and get stuck RIGHT HERE? This doesn't even scratch the surface of the level of faith you've demonstrated in past seasons.

MAKE THE MOVE!

If not now, then when? Start believing NOW! Get out of your own way. I decree that the voices of your circumstances are silenced.

Hebrews 11:1 **Now faith is the substance of things hoped for, the evidence of things not seen.**

DAY 6
Supernatural Supply Is Your Portion!

I decree resources and supernatural supply be released on your behalf! Lack and insufficiency has no place in your life. Command your day from the high place, not your need.

***Philippians 4:19* But my God shall supply all your need according to his riches in glory by Christ Jesus.**

***Psalms 23:1* A Psalm of David. The LORD is my shepherd; I shall not want.**

DAY 7
You Will Finish Strong!

I really sense an awakening of something on the inside of you. Not sure of what the spiritual climate currently is in your life, but something is brewing and God is definitely shifting, aligning and preparing you for something *"MAJOR"*. Get ready for a strong finish!

Philippians 1:6 **Being confident of this very thing, that he which hath begun a good work in you will perform it until the day of Jesus Christ.**

DAY 8
Integrity Has To Be Priority!

God can use you; but can he trust you? Perfect your integrity and master your character in this season. Make yourself a presentation unto God daily. Let holiness, righteousness and purity be intentional.

Romans 12:1-2

[1] I beseech you therefore, brethren, by the mercies of God, that ye present your bodies a living sacrifice, holy, acceptable unto God, which is your reasonable service.

[2] And be not conformed to this world: but be ye transformed by the renewing of your mind, that ye may prove what is that good, and acceptable, and perfect, will of God.

DAY 9
You're Loaded!

Psalms 68:19 **Blessed be the Lord, who daily loadeth us with benefits, even the God of our salvation. Selah.**

You are always on the heart and mind of the Father! He has made provisions for your safety and well being by loading you with some amazing benefits. Don't allow this to be another season that you leave precious resources on the table intended to shoot you into divine purpose! The heart of God is turned towards those whom He loves; I decree that you are one of them.

6 Benefits God Loads Us With Daily

1. Forgiveness of all iniquities
2. Healing from all diseases
3. Redemption from destruction
4. Crown of loving kindness & tender mercies
5. Satisfaction with good things
6. Righteousness & judgment executed on your behalf.

Psalms 103:1-5

[1] A Psalm of David. Bless the LORD, O my soul: and all that is within me, bless his holy name.

[2] Bless the LORD, O my soul, and forget not all his benefits:

[3] Who forgives all thine iniquities; who healeth all thy diseases;

[4] Who redeemed thy life from destruction; who crowned thee with lovingkindness and tender mercies;

[5] Who satisfied thy mouth with good things; so that thy youth is renewed like the eagle's.

DAY 10
Adopt A Breakthrough Mindset!

You must be willing to confront, challenge and oppose wicked authorities that possess what you're in pursuit of! Perseverance is a must because often times what we need or are in pursuit of won't come without resistance. Passion won't let you be passive! There has to be a measure of perseverance that you as a believer must operate in and live by. Do stop until it manifest!

- ❖ **Perseverance only focus is results.**
- ❖ **Perseverance has an appetite for breakthrough.**

Having a breakthrough mindset is a must! Let your perseverance hit your opposition like a hammer until your resistance turns into release.

Jeremiah 23:29 **Is not my word like as a fire? saith the LORD; and like a hammer that breaketh the rock in pieces?**

DAY 11
Contentment Is The Key!

One of the biggest hindrances to becoming persistent is the ability to be content. The enemy knows if he can keep you unstable emotionally and void of contentment, there are 3 things you will never be able to do:

1. Gain access to the things of God
2. Learn the things of God
3. Develop in the things of God

Philippians 4:11 KJV

Not that I speak in respect of want: for I have learned, in whatsoever state I am, therewith to be content.

DAY 12
A Time Of Completion!

It's so natural to gravitate to and focus on:

- ❖ **The absence of people**
- ❖ **The lack of finances & resources**
- ❖ **The need for opportunities**

Often we get stuck during times that God has ordained and designed to trim the fat off of our lives to make us lean. There is a work that God has started in you; trust his plan knowing He will finish it. Don't allow your focus to be shifted by the absence of, lack of, or the need of!

PHILIPPIANS 1:6 AMP

I am convinced and confident of this very thing, that He who has begun a good work in you will [continue to] perfect and complete it until the day of Christ Jesus [the time of His return].

Day 13
Submit To What He's Doing!

When you submit to the Lord's processing you'll always find yourself becoming more:

- ❖ **Efficient**
- ❖ **Effective**
- ❖ **Enduring**

All three are solid attributes and characteristics that come directly as a result of being processed and developed by The Father.

JAMES 1:4 AMP

And let endurance have its perfect result and do a thorough work, so that you may be perfect and completely developed [in your faith], lacking in nothing.

Day 14
Set Your Mind On The Right Things!

During times of accessing, learning and developing, it's important that you see the moves of God differently. You must learn to ask God the RIGHT questions.

Father what are you doing in me?

Father what are you revealing to me?

Father what are you stripping off me?

COLOSSIANS 3:2 AMP

Set your mind and keep focused habitually on the things above [the heavenly things], not on things that are on the earth [which have only temporal value].

Day 15
Do The Right Thing!

Don't get tired of doing the right thing. When God sees fit you will reap a harvest from the seeds you've planted.

Many times we get off track in life, not because of losing focus or lack of focus, but due to wrong focus. Things consume our personal resources and begin to cause our purpose behind doing things to be distorted.

What's your fuel?

What's your real motivation?

What's the driving force behind what you do?

Galatians 6:9 **So, we should not stop doing what is good. We should not get tired of it. If we do not get tired, then we shall receive a good result at the proper time.**

Day 16
What's Your "WHY"?

There has to be a shift in your "WHY"

Why you do what you do has to be redefined!

Whoever controls your "WHY" controls your peace, joy and encouragement; that's who you'll be drawn to for affirmation and validation. There's a dimension of pressing that you must operate in BECAUSE OF & IN SPITE OF. It cannot be people driven but must be God centered. This will cause the things of God to truly manifest in your life.

Purpose- The reason for which something is done or created, the basis on which something exist.

Colossians 3:23 **whatever things you do, do them for the Lord. Do them as well as you can for him. Do not work only for people.**

Day 17
Have You Responded To That Word Yet?

RECEIVING THE WORD OF THE LORD CONSIST OF 3 THINGS:

1. Listening

(Not just hearing or not speaking out of respect/courtesy)

2. Submitting

(Intentionally coming under the authority of that word)

3. Obeying

(Do what's required of you whether you like it or not)

Jeremiah 33:14 **Behold, the days come, saith the LORD, that I will perform that good thing which I have promised unto the house of Israel and to the house of Judah.**

Day 18
Embrace Correction And Make The Adjustment!

When it comes to change, especially for the better, we have to fully embrace the fact that corrective actions are a major part of the process.

- ❖ Correction doesn't always mean that something is wrong.
- ❖ Correction doesn't always mean you're wrong.
- ❖ Correction doesn't always mean you did or are doing something wrong.

Psalms 15:32 **He that refuseth instruction despiseth his own soul: but he that heareth reproof getteth understanding**

Day 19
Keep It Real With Yourself!

Oftentimes life requires self-assessments because what you're doing and/or how you're doing it is not efficient or does not have the maximum effectiveness needed.

- ❖ How does your position fit into the grand scheme of things?
- ❖ Does your approach, perspective or method comply with the vision, expectations or assignment you as an individual are being held accountable to?

Never make it a habit of trying to rally folk around you that will endorse your feelings or point of view; gather those who challenge you and hold you accountable.

***Psalms 51:6* Behold, thou desirest truth in the inward parts: and in the hidden part thou shalt make me to know wisdom.**

Day 20
It's Ok To Tweak Some Things!

Your mindset concerning adjustments and enhancements must change in order to benefit fully from it.

- Correction must be received the right way.
- Correction is used to make "YOU" better not worse.
- Correction is used to make "THINGS" better not worse.
- Correction increases your capacity.
- Correction brings adjustments that break you through.
- Correction modifies and enhances.
- Correction unlocks what's been held up in your life.

Proverbs 15:10 KJV **Correction is grievous unto him that forsaketh the way: and he that hateth reproof shall die.**

Day 21
There's Always Room For Better!

You must understand that just because it's working for you does not mean it's working! It may be beneficial and prosperous for you, but is it beneficial and prosperous to God & His Kingdom.

- ❖ Sometimes things that are not broke still have to be fixed in order to bring them into compliance with the standards of God's Kingdom.

- ❖ It must be understood that BETTER comes as a result of Change being initiated by those in greater expectation.

Isaiah 43:19 **Behold, I will do a new thing; now it shall spring forth; shall ye not know it? I will even make a way in the wilderness, and rivers in the desert.**

Better is not limited to improvements made to what exist already; but it also encompasses new things being added to enhance or replace what's already there.

Day 22
Time To Live A Limitless Life!

If you are going to experience any real level of consistency, maturity and advancement in your life, you must be willing to embrace something that may totally destroy what you see absolutely nothing wrong with. Sometimes you've got to reflect on how God has been in previous seasons and let that change your perspective concerning your next.

Philippians 4:13 **I can do all things through Christ that strengthens me.**

1. **I Can= Absolutely no doubt.**

2. **Do All Things = No limits.**

3. **Through Christ = Unrestricted ability.**

4. **That strengthens me = Divinely enables me; to endow supernaturally.**

Limitless living starts with making specific personal adjustments with the future as your focus and motivation.

- ❖ **Change your Language -** Began to speak from a definitive place, not a place of compromise. "I Can Do All Things"!

- ❖ **Change your mindset** - Set your affection on things above, not on things on the earth. Colossians 3:2 KJV

- ❖ **Change your habits-** Delight thyself also in the Lord; and he shall give thee the desires of thine heart. Commit thy way unto the Lord; trust also in him; and he shall bring it to pass. Psalms 37:4-5 KJV

Limitless living requires you to consistently live with expectancy!

Day 23
Embrace The Potter's Wheel!

3 THINGS THAT THE POTTER'S WHEEL DOES FOR YOU

1. MARKS YOU WITH DISTINCTION

(Matt 7:16 You shall know them by the fruit that they bare)

2. STRENGTHENS YOU FOR OPPOSITION

(I Cor 15:58 Be ye steadfast, unmovable always abounding in the work of the Lord)

4. CULTIVATES YOU TO PRODUCE

(John 14:12 These works that I do ye shall do them also; and greater works shall you do)

- Pay the price now for the future you want to be in.
- Don't go through your process, grow through your process.
- You must know that your process is from God. Illegitimate talk will come from people who are not privy to the details of your process.

Don't abort the process because you mistake it for an attack! Stop binding and rebuking what God has ordained to get the best "YOU" out of "YOU"! This may not be a time ordained to bless you; it just may be a time to develop you.

Day 24
The Potential Of Prayer!

This is an hour where saints are committing to lives of prayer like never before; but many walk away with no clue that the quality of their life and life's style plays a major role in the Lord's position as it relates to their prayers.

***I Peter 3:12* For the eyes of the Lord are over the righteous, and his ears are open unto their prayers: but the face of the Lord is against them that do evil.**

<u>*Let's break this scripture down to fully embrace it.*</u>

- **The eyes** = Focus, attention. To take heed, *perceive
- **Perceive** = look on (someone or something) in a particular way; regard
- **Over** = Upon, directed towards
- **Righteous** = Equitable, innocent, Holy
- **Prayer** = petition: request, supplication. (Need, Want, A seeking)

<u>*There is tremendous power in right standings.*</u>

Keep your posture right towards God and maintain a life of righteousness. Right standings keep you on the mind of the Father!

Day 25
Spirit Of Fear
DECLARATION & CONFESSION

- **I RENOUNCE ALL FEAR, ANXIETY, PANIC, WORRY, MENTAL TORMENT AND DREAD.**

- I DECLARE GOD HAS NOT GIVEN ME THE SPIRIT OF FEAR BUT OF POWER, LOVE, AND A SOUND MIND.

- **I SEVER EVERY CORD AND KNOT OF FEAR THAT ATTACKS MY MIND AND MY ABILITY TO LOVE AND RECEIVE LOVE.**

- I COMMAND ALL DEMONS OF FEAR THAT CAUSE MENTAL, EMOTIONAL AND PHYSICAL TORMENT TO LOOSE MY MIND AND BODY NOW IN JESUS NAME.

- **I SPEAK VICTORY AND TOTAL RESTORATION FROM ALL FEAR IN THE NAME OF JESUS**

- I DECLARE HIS LOVE CAST OUT ALL MY FEARS. THERE IS NO FEAR IN LOVE, BUT PERFECT LOVE CASTETH OUT ALL FEAR; BECAUSE FEAR HAS TORMENT.

- **I BREAK COVENANT WITH FEAR.**

- I WILL NOT BE SHY, TIMID OR INTIMIDATED.

- **I DECLARE AND DECREE I STAND IN BOLD CONFIDENCE BACKED BY THE POWER OF THE HOLY GHOST!**

Day 26
Prayer And Decree Against
DEPRESSION & SUICIDE

Father I thank you that my life is free from ALL false weights, burdens and oppressive influence in the name of Jesus. Your word declares in John 8:36, "If the Son therefore shall make you free, ye shall be free indeed."

So, according to your word, I declare over my life that I AM FREE from all emotional instability and mental heaviness in the name of Jesus. Father according to Philippians 4:6-7, "I worry about NOTHING and confess that your peace that passes all understanding guards my heart and mind through Jesus Christ!"

Depression is not my portion and has no authority or control over my life. I exercise my authority over it according to Luke 10:19 where you give me power to tread upon serpents & scorpions and over all the power of the enemy and nothing shall harm.

So Father according to II Corinthians 10:5, I cast down every imagination & high thing that exalts itself against the knowledge of you; I bring my thoughts, feelings & emotions into captivity to the authority of Jesus Christ. Father thank you that I walk in total freedom from DEPRESSION, SADNESS, LOW SELF ESTEEM, LONELINESS, INFERIORITY, SELF DESTRUCTIVE THINKING & SUICIDAL THOUGHTS/TENDENCIES!

Day 27
Scriptures And Decrees For FOCUS

Spend time today reading, meditating and praying the following scriptures.

Philippians 4:8
Finally, brethren, whatsoever things are true, whatsoever things are honest, whatsoever things are just, whatsoever things are pure, whatsoever things are lovely, whatsoever things are of good report; if there be any virtue, and if there be any praise, think on these things.

Joshua 1:9
Have not I commanded thee? Be strong and of a good courage; be not afraid, neither be thou dismayed: for the Lord thy God is with thee whithersoever thou goest.

Decree & Confess The Following:

John 10:10 I am aware that the thief cometh not but for to kill steal and destroy.

I Corinthians 15:58 I will be steadfast, unmovable always abounding in your work Lord.

Philippians 4:6 I will be anxious for nothing; your peace will guard my heart and my mind.

Isaiah 26:3 I decree you wilt keep me in perfect peace; my mind is stayed on you: because I trust in you.

Colossians 3:2 My affections are set on things above and not on things on this earth.

Day 28
Authority!

Matthew 16:19 And I will give unto thee the keys of the kingdom of heaven: and whatsoever thou shalt bind on earth shall be bound in heaven: and whatsoever thou shalt loose on earth shall be loosed in heaven.

Keys = Unlimited Access; Authority

Matthew 18:18 Verily I say unto you, whatsoever ye shall bind on earth shall be bound in heaven: and whatsoever ye shall loose on earth shall be loosed in heaven.

1. **The backing of the Kingdom**
2. **The resources of the Kingdom**
3. **The authority of the Kingdom**

Day 29
Prayer Is Your Foundation!

Prayer is the foundation of every successful Christian endeavor. Time spent with God is vital if you desire a fruitful Christian life.

Prayer is not an emotional release or an escape valve. It is much more than just asking God for a favor. Prayer is not a religious exercise. You should be getting results each time you pray. In order to get results in prayer, you must be convinced that God wants to answer your prayers.

<u>God responds to faith not words.</u>

Matthew 21:22 KJV **And all things, whatsoever ye shall ask in prayer, believing, ye shall receive.**

Matthew 6:7 **"But when ye pray, use not vain repetitions, as the heathen do: for they think that they shall be heard for their much speaking.**

Day 30
Birth Your Own!

There's a God ordained process that's designed to prepare you and launch you.

"Give them their baby back!" What's ordained for you is inside of you! You're frustrated because you've taken ownership, custody and responsibility for something that was birthed out of someone else's process.

Jeremiah 29:11 For I know the thoughts that I think toward you, saith the LORD, thoughts of peace, and not of evil, to give you an expected end. You can't jump from hearing the plans of God for your life right into receiving the manifestation.

There is a place between hearing the plans of God concerning your life and the manifestation of the plans of God concerning your life called **THE PROCESS**.

PROCESS = A series of actions or steps taken and endured to achieve a specific result. The process is a REQUIRED & NECESSARY component God uses to polish and build us!

PHILIPPIANS 1:6 AMP I am convinced and confident of this very thing, that He who has begun a good work in you will [continue to] perfect and complete it until the day of Christ Jesus [the time of His return].

IT IS NEVER ABOUT WHEN YOU FEEL YOU'RE READY; IT'S ALWAYS ABOUT WHEN GOD KNOWS HE CAN TRUST YOU!

As you have been challenged and stretched for the last 30 days, allow this to be a time of self-assessment, personal adjustments and realignment. I decree that your NEXT has arrived and the only potential hindrance to your best days is you! My desire is that you be challenged in a new way to walk out God's absolute best for you and your future in Him.

~ Apostle James D. Holiday, Sr.

Power Points for Today's Busy Believer

I'M
CHANGING
MY STATUS
Available at
amazon
Get Your Copy Today
Or can be purchased via
www.paypal.me/JDHMinistries
PayPal

EMBRACING THE NEW YOU
JAMES D. HOLIDAY SR.
EMBRACING THE NEW YOU
by James D. Holiday Sr.
GET YOUR COPY TODAY
Available at
amazon.com
OR CAN BE PURCHASED VIA
WWW.PAYPAL.ME/JDHMINISTRIES

Made in the USA
Monee, IL
03 May 2020